AF408417

Published by Enna's Press
ISBN: 979-8-9945-835-5-5

Library of Congress Control Number: 2026904755

Art & Design: Created using licensed assets from Canva Pro.

For more books by the author, visit : iqralittlepages.com

JUVENILE NONFICTION / Places / Africa
JUVENILE NONFICTION / Social Science / Customs, Traditions, Anthropology

Printed in USA. First Edition 2026.

Note to Parents & Educators

Dear Grown-ups,

A child's first sense of pride often starts with a simple truth: "*This is where I come from*".

For every child, knowing their roots is a powerful gift. This book is a joyful celebration of Ghana's story; its ground, its gifts, and its people. It is designed to nurture a child's sense of belonging, appreciation, and confidence in their heritage. We invite your little one to:

- See the beauty in their culture.
- Feel a deep connection to their roots.
- Know that their story is a proud part of a larger, vibrant tapestry.

Our hope is that these pages spark proud conversations filled with love, identity, and shared pride.

Discover more books for curious toddlers at : iqralittlepages.com

Happy exploring and growing together!

Sherifa E. Cudjoe
Author & Parent

For Mawunyo

MY HERITAGE PLATE

THIS BOOK BELONGS TO:

A PROUD CHILD FROM THE

---------------------------------- REGION OF GHANA.

MY FAVORITE GHANAIAN WORD IS:

(It means: _______________________________________)

This is Africa. Our big, beautiful continent. Long ago, the first stories began here. On Africa's sunny west coast...a black star shines bright

That star is our home. Ghana. A name that means "Warrior King", strong and brave. We look small on the map, but mighty in spirit. Our symbol is the Black Star. It is a light for all of Africa.

Ghana is never alone. To the **West**, we say *Bonjour* to **Cote d'Ivoire**. To the **North**, we share the sun with **Burkina Faso**. To the **East**, we say *Bonjour* again to **Togo** and to the **South**, we greet our friend, the mighty Atlantic Ocean. We are a good neighbor in a family of nations.

This is where my feet touch the earth. This is where my story begins. I stand on the soil of my ancestors. I stand proud.

Our soil is a treasure chest. For centuries, it has given the world gold. This gold is our strength. It is in our history and in our future.

Our land grows the cocoa bean. This little bean
brings joy to the whole world as chocolate.
We are the keepers of this sweetness.

From our mighty lands comes the shea tree.
Its nut gives us shea butter. It softens, heals, and
protects. It is the care of our mothers, made into
cream.

13

Our Atlantic Ocean does not divide us; it feeds us. It gives fish for our plates and energy for our dreams. It is powerful, like our people.

Gold nugget

Cocoa pod

Shea butter

Silver fish

Look at all the gifts from our lands! Gold from the earth, cocoa from the forest, shea from the Savannah, fish from the sea. Each one is different and each one is needed.

Look at our people! We speak with many voices: Ga, Twi, Nzema, Fante, Dagbani, Ewe, and more. We wear many colors. But our smiles speak the same language: *Welcome. We are home.*

Sixteen (16) regions: Ashanti, Greater Accra, Central, Western, Eastern, Volta, Northern, Upper East, Upper West, Bono, Ahafo, Bono East, Oti, Savannah, North East, Western North. Different threads. One people. One Ghana.

This gold, this cocoa, this shea, this fish, this land, this people, this pride - it is all yours. You have inherited a kingdom of riches. These are the tools for your hands. You can taste sweetness. You can feel the strength. You are part of this story.

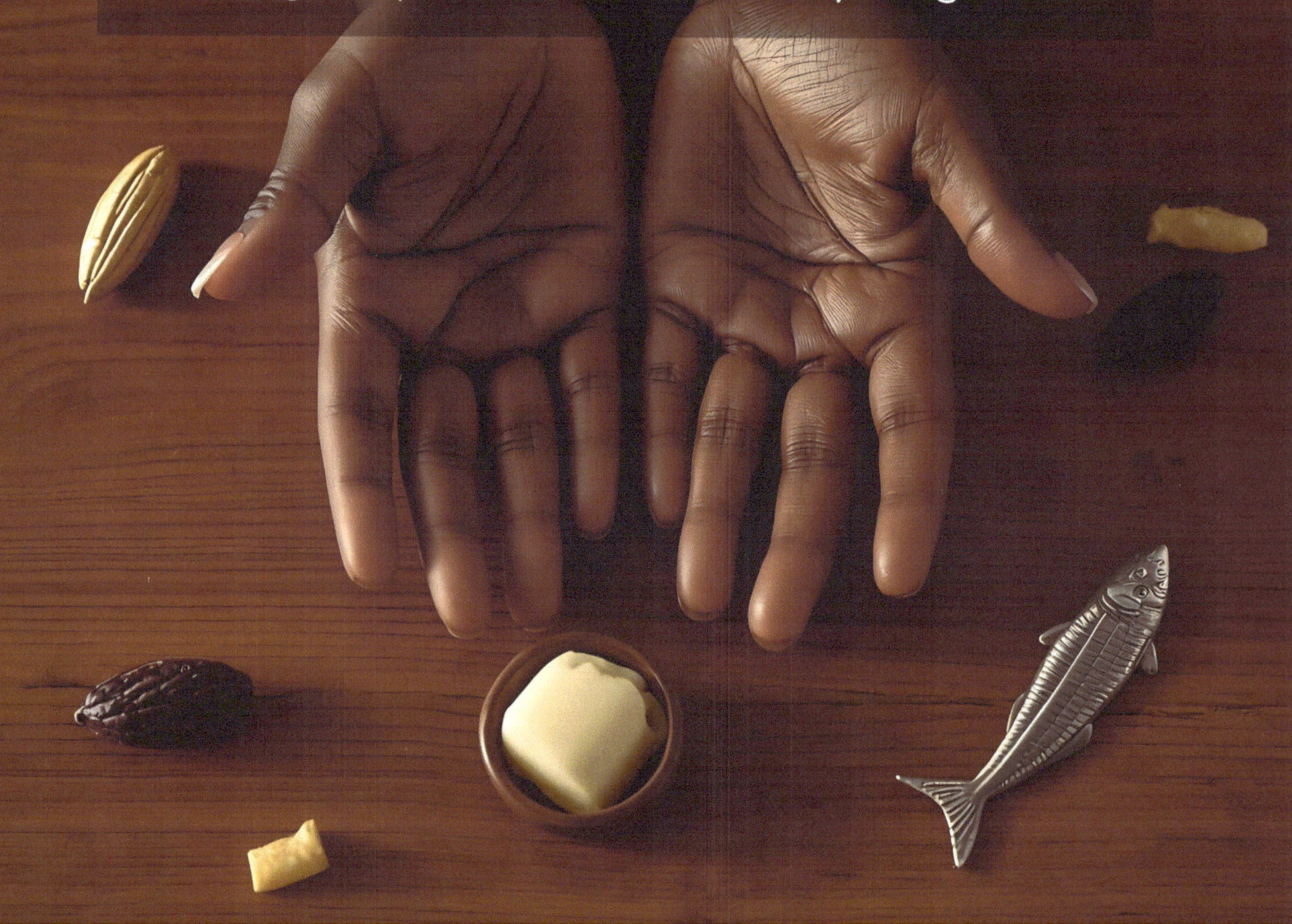

These are your hands. What will you hold? What will you build? What will you heal? With these gifts, your hands can do anything.

You will build with them. You will heal with them.
You will create with them. You will lead with them.
You are the next star. Walk tall, little one.
The future is yours.

20

My soil. My wealth. My people. My pride.
I am Ghana

MY FAMILY'S STORY

This is our country. This is home.

With your grown-up, find Mama's region. Papa's region. Grandma's. Grandpa's.

Trace them with your fingers

Each one is a part of your story.

Our family comes from:

----------------------- , ----------------------- , ----------------------- , -----------------

Little one,
You have seen your gold.
You have met your people.
You have traced your land.

Now go.
Play in the sun.
Help at the table.
Listen to the stories.
Ask questions.
Grow strong and kind.

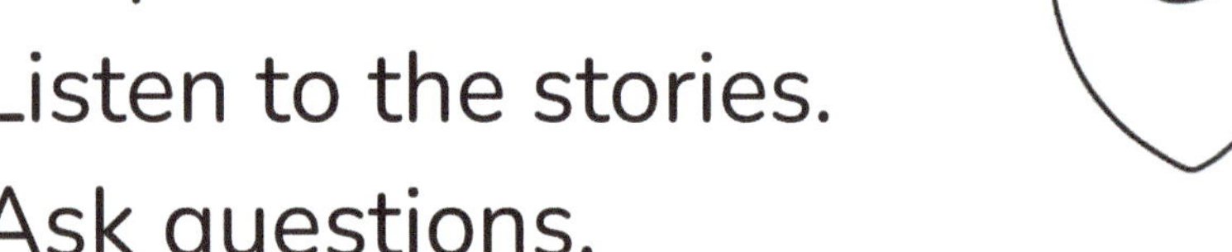

Your roots are deep.
Your wings are growing.
And always, always remember:

You belong here.
You are Ghana and Ghana is proud of you.